Fat Burning Smoothies

Easy Smoothie Recipes for Burning Fat and Losing Weight Fast

Donna Hardin

© 2013 by Donna Hardin

ISBN-13: 978-1492923787

ISBN-10: 1492923788

All Rights Reserved. No part of this publication may be reproduced in any form or by any means, including scanning, photocopying, or otherwise without prior written permission of the copyright holder.

First Printing, 2013

Printed in the United States of America

Fat Burning Smoothies

Easy Smoothie Recipes for Burning Fat and Losing Weight Fast

The purpose of this book is to educate you as best as possible on the topic of smoothies and how to burn fat and lose weight using a smoothie diet. All the information included in this book has been carefully researched and checked for accuracy.

However, I am not a certified doctor so I cannot guarantee nor imply that the information contained herein is appropriate for every individual, situation or purpose. Although I tried to include as much information as possible, some omissions or errors might exist, for which I cannot be held responsible.

The reader assumes the risk and full responsibility for all actions, and the author will not be held responsible for any loss or damage, whether consequential, incidental, special or otherwise that may result from the information presented in this publication.

I have relied on my own experience as well as different sources to write this book, and I have done my best to check facts and to give credit where it is due.

Thank you for understanding.

Table of Contents

Introduction 7

Why are Smoothies So Powerful? 9

The Big Misconception about Fat Burning and Weight Loss 15

    Smoothies, Fat Loss and Weight Loss 17

    The Biology Behind Fat loss and Weght Loss 19

    The Risks Nobody Talks About 21

    How Fast Can You See Results? 22

Fat Burning Diet 25

    Who Can Do It and How Long? 27

    Food Consumption during a Smoothie Diet 28

Fat Burning Smoothie Recipes 31

    Vegetable Smoothies 33

    Fruit Smoothies 47

    Green Smoothies 66

    Mix-Match Smoothie Recipes 83

Final Recommendations 97

About the Author 101

Introduction

I want to start this book by saying that I've been exactly where you are right now. I know how it is to feel hopeless about my body and my weight. I know how frustrating it can be to try countless weight loss products, diets and fitness routines, but nothing seems to work.

But I tell you this: Don't give up because I didn't – and I am living, breathing proof that weight loss can be achieved naturally. Whether you want to lose weight for health reasons, start a healthier lifestyle or simply feel more beautiful, I dedicate this book to you.

You see, being an only child, I grew up a spoiled brat. I would do what I wanted and eat what I wanted – and all I wanted to do back then was bury myself in romance novels and junk food. As a result, for most of my young life, I was overweight.

My life was at its lowest when I turned 27. I lived alone, I was sickly and I was 30 pounds overweight. To make matters worse, I lost my job because I felt depressed and unmotivated. This is when I decided to get up from the sofa.

For many months, I tried several diets, went to the gym and consulted with many nutritionists. I would lose weight but then eventually gain it back. But I didn't give up. And I was right not to because shortly after, a friend recommended that I try a green smoothie fast. I didn't think twice about trying it because well, who doesn't love smoothies?

It changed my life. These glasses of nutritious goodness made me realize that healthy food can be equally or even more delicious than junk food, so why choose the latter if what you're getting out of it is not in any way good for your health?

Over the next months, I gradually lost the extra pounds, my immune system became stronger and I realized I'd never felt better in my life. I had my life back and I promised myself there was no way to go but up.

To this day, I feel like I owe my health to my first glass of smoothie. That's why I am sharing my story with you.

If you are in a similar situation now as I was in the past, let my story and this book guide you back to the right path of health. It's never too late to make peace with your body and give it what it truly deserves.

So if you're ready, let us begin our journey and hopefully in the end, you'll also be saying "Smoothies changed my life."

Why are Smoothies So Powerful?

Because you are here with me in the first chapter, it means that you've decided to lose weight the healthy way so, congratulations!

Drinking smoothies is life's way of giving us a treat – it's like having a healthy meal and dessert all in one glass. Healthy smoothies are also an easy way to get your daily dose of fruits and vegetables, especially if you're not fond of them.

Here are the most common health benefits of drinking smoothies:

A Good Source of Vitamins and Minerals

Drinking fruit and vegetable smoothies is an efficient way to get your much-needed vitamins and minerals. Since they are in liquid form, your body absorbs these nutrients much faster when compared to eating produce the traditional way.

There are mainly 6 categories of fruit, all of which you can include in your smoothies:

1. Berries have powerful antioxidant and anti-inflammatory properties. They also contain phytonutrients that help fight diseases. Aside from all the berries you can think of such as blueberries, blackberries, cranberries, raspberries and strawberries, grapes also fall under this category.

2. Citrus fruits are rich in Vitamin C, folate and potassium. Grapefruits, oranges, lemons and tangerines belong to this group.

3. Drupes are packed with beta-carotene which promotes healthy eye and immune system function. They are also rich sources of Vitamin C and potassium. Apricots, cherries, peaches and plums are the most common drupe fruits.

4. Melons are not only delicious, but they're nutritious as well. They are rich in Vitamin C. Cantaloupes, casabas, honey dews and watermelons belong to the melons category.

5. Pomes are packed full of Vitamin C and potassium. Apples and pears are the most common members of this category.

6. Tropical fruits promote bone, nerve and thyroid gland health. They also play a big role in keeping the body's blood sugar levels in check. These flavorful fruits contain high amounts of Vitamin C, folate, manganese and potassium. Examples of tropical fruits include avocados, bananas, coconuts, kiwis, mangoes, pineapples and pomegranates.

Veggies, on the other hand, also provide an amazing roster of vitamins, minerals and other important nutrients. Leafy greens are at the top of the list because they contain chlorophyll which purifies the blood, rejuvenates the body and strengthens the immune system. They are also rich in Vitamins A, C and K, B Vitamins, calcium, iron, potassium, phosphorus, magnesium, manganese, zinc and more!

A Good Source of Fiber

Fiber promotes healthy digestion and maintains healthy levels of blood sugar and blood cholesterol in the body. The recommended daily intake of fiber is 20 grams for ladies and 30 grams for the gents.

One serving of fruit contains 2-4 grams of fiber. Some fruit, like apples, blackberries and pears provides up to 5-7 grams per serving. When you combine 4-5 different fruits and vegetables into one glass of smoothie, you will instantly meet the recommended daily amount of fiber.

Now, this brings us to the difference between juicing and blending.

Juicing is extracting the juice out of fresh fruits and vegetables, making no use of the pulp or the flesh part. On the other hand, blending makes use of the whole fruit and vegetable, simply blending them together into one healthy drink.

Because of this, drinking smoothies allows you to retain and consume the produce's natural fiber content, unlike when you drink fresh fruit and vegetable juices, which contain no fiber.

Don't get me wrong, I have nothing against fresh juices. In fact, I like to alternate juicing and blending as part of my diet, as they are both beneficial. But since we are talking about fiber right now, I'd say that smoothies win this one.

Increase Your Intake of Fruits and Vegetables

Fruits are the easy part. If you're not a fan of vegetables, then drinking smoothies allows you to consume the recommended amount of vegetables in one glass.

The best part is, you can barely taste them. This allows you to get nutrients from produce you don't normally eat. If you have an issue with the way certain veggies taste, you can easily mask the taste with a fruit or two.

According to the Harvard School of Public Health, a minimum of 9 servings of fruits and vegetables per day is recommended to stay healthy – and this can easily be achieved through drinking smoothies.

Promote Clear and Healthy Skin

Your skin reflects what you eat. More so, the state of your skin mirrors the state of your body. If you regularly eat nutritious foods and your body is healthy, there's a big chance that you have healthy skin, too. Apart from the multitude of skin-friendly nutrients you gain from eating fruits and veggies, smoothies are also extremely hydrating. This helps prevent skin dryness which is a sign of unhealthy skin.

Smoothies also have detoxification properties which allows your body to get rid of toxins and other impurities the proper way, instead of through your skin, which causes breakouts.

Allow You to Get Creative with Your Diet

No matter what anybody says, you're going to eat what you want to eat – and blending gives you this kind of freedom. You can choose fruit-vegetable combinations according to your personal taste. There are also countless smoothie base options – from water, low-fat milk, low-fat yogurt, to soy milk and many more.

Mix and match and get creative! There are literally thousands of smoothie recipes out there and later in this book, I will share with you my personal favorites as well as my very own concoctions.

The Big Misconception about Fat Burning and Weight Loss

One huge mistake that people make while on a certain diet or exercise routine is not being able to distinguish between burning fat and actually losing weight. This mistake alone frequently prevents people from reaching their fitness goals.

So, to answer our all-important first question, what is the difference between fat loss and weight loss?

To explain, weight loss basically refers to losing pounds on a scale. You have to remember that the lost weight doesn't take into account whether you've lost muscle or fat, or whether you look significantly different because of the weight loss.

Fat loss, on the other hand, is a different story. It doesn't depend on the numbers on the scale, but rather on losing so-called flab and specific inches, and looking different in appearance due to the fat loss.

Losing weight without losing fat is not a good plan. When you do that, you must lose muscle. When you eat fewer calories than you burn per day, your body must then use reserved or stored energy so it can continue to function properly. These reserves can be drawn from either, fat or muscle.

Now, if you do not use the correct method for losing fat, you will confuse your body and it will burn muscle for energy instead of fat. This error will show in how you look in the mirror. You may have lost pounds when you check the scale, but your appearance will not be much different as the flab and fat on your body remain, leaving you with a less attractive figure.

This is usually where the term "skinny-fat" comes in. Skinny-fat is indicated by a thin stature, but with a saggy stomach, arm fat, etc. People who unintentionally lose muscle instead of fat may see their weight go down a good bit, but still look as described. Always remember that if you want to have a good-looking body, *lose fat, not muscle*.

When you follow the proper strategies to lose fat, you won't quickly see a big change on the scale. This is because muscle is way heavier than fat. Don't worry though, because the difference will show in your body shape and physique and actually, in how your body feels.

If you lose fat, though, you can maintain the same weight but your body will look very different. Two people can be the same height and weight, but still look completely different. That's why weight loss alone can be unreliable.

The reason is there are many factors that dictate weight loss or gain, such as food choices t, water loss or retention, etc. The difference between two people with the same height and weight who look different is the percentage of fat they have on their bodies.

One factor that can positively influence whether you experience weight loss or fat loss is the delicious and healthy treat called the Smoothie.

Smoothies, Fat Loss and Weight Loss

At this point you may be wondering, how can smoothies help me when it comes to burning fat and losing weight?

To start with, let's focus on the two types of smoothies commonly used for weight loss purposes: fruit smoothies and green smoothies (made with a mix of fruits and vegetables).

It is important to note that while you can lose fat or weight on smoothies alone, you could try to substitute smoothies for one or two meals a day, or in place of a snack during the first few days to help you transition to an all-smoothie diet.

When you include smoothies in your diet at the beginning, you will have a tasty and satisfying fiber and nutrient-rich meal that also satisfies your body's need for hydration, while keeping your calorie intake at an all-time low.

One mistake that can really ruin your dream body efforts is thinking that your yummy smoothie is an after meal drink. Stop right there. While most smoothies indeed contain low calorie levels, you must make sure that if you add them into your diet, you do not add them to your existing meals.

The explanation for this is that if you just add smoothies to your existing diet, you will not burn fat or lose weight. Instead, you will build fat and add more weight. Never forget that smoothies must be considered as replacement meals and not add-ons.

So how do you get the most out of the smoothies?

Use smoothies to bring your caloric intake down as far as you safely can. You want to keep the volume of food you consume about the same to avoid problems with excessive hunger. This way, you can basically eat as much as you are used to, but you consume way fewer calories than you feel.

You can do this by exchanging some of the sweeter and higher sugar content ingredients you would normally include in your smoothie for green leafy vegetables. For example, if you concoct a smoothie that contains an entire banana, you could easily just use one-half of the banana (high calories-per volume) and substitute an apple (medium calories-per-volume) in place of the banana. Or, try using a handful of spinach (low calories-per-volume) instead. Now that makes a huge difference.

The Biology Behind Fat Loss and Weght Loss

During Weight Loss

When you lose weight, water, lean body mass and stored fat go along with it. You're going to need to replace lost water in your body, so be sure to keep yourself well-hydrated while you are dieting. This is good for your health because when you lose fat, your body needs to maintain a steady metabolic rate, and water helps that.

Here are the goals:

In the early weeks of weight loss, a minimum of 75% of the weight you lose should be fat loss, and not more than 25% should come from lean body mass.

As you continue to lose weight, especially if you include certain types of exercise in your weight loss plan, fat loss should be about 90% of the weight you lose and lean body mass should be about 10%.

During Fat Loss

According to Centers for Disease Control and Preventon, 66% of Americans are obese. With these high numbers, people tend to focus only on losing weight and not fat. As I've emphasized to you in this entire chapter, go for the fat first. If you do, what happens inside your body?

The simple answer is that when you focus on losing fat by eating fat-burning foods or through exercise, your body turns your excess stored fat into very usable forms of energy, shrinking your fat cells.

To illustrate, compare your fat loss goal to a destination you want to reach by car. In this scenario, your body is the car and the amount of body energy you use is equal to how fast you can get to your destination. So when you sit around just watching TV and the like, less energy is used, therefore it will take more time to reach your destination. But if you work out, more body energy is used, therefore you get to your destination much faster.

In short, the more exercise you do, the more energy is used and the more fat cells are burned.

The Risks Nobody Talks About

People who are trying to lose weight go through extraordinary efforts in dieting and exercising to reach their goal. It"s easy to overdo it in an unhealthy way that you can't maintain as an actual change in your lifestyle.

For example, you probably didn't know that experts recommend you should lose only one to two pounds per week maximum. Of course, you'll say that at that slow pace, it would take you too long to reach your goal, but the pace at which you lose weight can actually greatly influence your long-term progress.

Keep in mind that a pound of fat, which is about 0.45 Kg, contains 3500 calories. This means that to lose a pound a week, you need to burn 500 more calories than you consume per day. (3500 calories = 7 days x 500 calories)

Also, if you lose a lot of weight very quickly, it may not be fat that you're losing. It might be water weight or even lean tissue, since it's hard to burn that many fat calories in a short period. In some cases, though, faster weight loss can be safe if it's done the right way.

To help you understand better, let me explain what water weight loss is. When you're on a diet, whether a smoothie fast or something else, what you consume is low in calories. Because of this, your body releases and makes use of a carbohydrate called glycogen, which is stored in your muscles and liver. Glycogen is known to hold on to water, so when the body releases its store of the carbohydrate, the water it is holding is also released.

This results to a drop in weight and usually happens during the first few days of calorie restriction. Most dieters mistake water weight loss with real weight loss but in fact, water weight will be gained back as soon as your normal diet resumes.

But there are instances when quick weight loss can be achieved. For example, doctors might prescribe very low calorie diets for rapid weight loss if obesity is causing serious health problems. But an extreme diet like this requires medical supervision.

So ladies, what I'm basically telling you here is that real weight loss takes a lot of patience – losing weight too fast is the biggest hindrance you can have to achieving a leaner, healthier body.

How Fast Can You See Results?

Losing fat is gradual. It will begin to show in your appearance in as little as a week or two weeks. To achieve that, you need to strictly follow the changes you've made in your diet and exercise plans. The slower, yet more effective process of fat burning needs discipline if you want to see results at all.

You can't actually pin-point where you will shed fat, or how fast you'll get your results. It's different for every individual. Weight loss and fat loss don't work like a point-and-shoot game.

For example, CT scans, dexa scans and MRIs that use X-ray beams to measure body composition have never shown any evidence to prove spot reduction is possible .

According to Boston University School of Medicine's Boston Obesity and Nutrition Research Center director, Susan Fried, when we lose weight, we do it all over in exactly the proportion that's distributed throughout our body.

Coaches will say don't strength/weight-train when you're trying to lose weight. Despite the potential for weight gain associated with strength training, individuals who regularly perform these exercises typically improve their body composition, or ratio of lean tissue to fat.

According to the President's Council on Physical Fitness and Sports, having a healthy lean-to-fat ratio is a good indicator of overall physical fitness, and provides a better gauge of your general health than simply weighing less than you did before.

Always, always consult your doctor and a nutritionist for more information about losing fat by changing your diet. Consult your doctor and a fitness specialist for more information about fat loss through exercise.

Fat Burning Diet

Now that we have discussed the basics of what a smoothie is and how it can help you lose weight, let's move on to how you can apply what you just learned to your actual diet.

It is popularly known that smoothies are a good staple in anyone's diet, whether you want to lose fat or simply want to consume extra nutrients. What do you do first, though, to start your very own fat-burning smoothie diet plan?

First, weigh yourself on the morning of your first day before you shower but after you use the bathroom. This will give you your body's resting weight. Then, you can start with the smoothies.

The fiber, fruits, vegetables, protein and the like in smoothies will help you increase your metabolism. Depending on the recipe, smoothies will also provide healthy fats to help you burn fat.

Combine exercise and smoothies and you will reap the benefits in no time. Good exercise and a good smoothie diet will help your body reach its optimal performance potential by burning unnecessary fat naturally.

Pre-work out: About an hour before, drink a smoothie with fruit ingredients and include grains like soaked oats. (see the Cherry Oatmeal Delight recipe) Also add a tablespoon of coconut oil and protein powder. Fruits and oats are generally low in fat and carbohydrates which means they are easy to digest, but still provide the fuel you need when working out.

Consuming a pre-workout meal in the form of a smoothie is an efficient way to gain energy and protect your muscles during exercise routines.

Post-Workout: Right after finishing your last set, immediately drink a protein and fruit smoothie. This should include high-protein plants like flax seeds, which will help your muscles directly absorb the protein. (See the Green Smoothie for the Newbie and Smoothie Zing recipes).

On the other hand, the fruits' simple sugars will replenish the glycogen you lost during exercise. If you're into heavy lifting, go ahead and sip the smoothie during your work out. It is best to pick fruits that are easy to digest like apples, bananas, berries and peaches(See the Apple Cucumber Twist, Berry Nutty Peach and Blue Banana Smoothie recipes).

Drinking a glass of smoothie after working out will provide your body with nutrients essential for optimal growth and recuperation.

Who Can Do It and How Long?

Well, if you're asking what the qualifications are to be cleared to start a smoothie diet, here is the quick and simple answer:

"Anyone who is trying to lose weight and has no medical conditions can follow the diet with caution. Start slow at first and then alter your lifestyle as you go - that is the key to healthy living. Simply put, "Following this plan for a couple of weeks to boost weight loss is great but one should not follow it too long," explains Priya Kathpal, an online Nutrition Consultant and Dietician.

Now for the second question: How long you should go on a fat-burning smoothie diet depends on how many fresh fruits and vegetables and other fat burning foods you put in your system versus how much unhealthy, processed or "junk" food and fat you eat. The more junk food you eat, the more frequently you will need to go on a smoothie fast to maintain a normal weight. So part of the solution is to remove as much junk food as possible from your diet,

The point is to balance your diet and stay healthy. Some people like to do a range of four days to one week about four times a year, per season. Some people do more. Remember, balance is key to this challenge.

Food Consumption during a Smoothie Diet

You can choose to still eat regular food during your first smoothie diet. Although most people prefer to go full-smoothie even on the first day, you can add whole foods or make an interchangeable meal plan.

Like I said earlier, I would personally recommend incorporating solid food into your smoothie diet during the first few days, especially if you're a beginner, so that you will experience a smooth transition in between diets.

When you combine smoothies and healthy foods, you get the fat loss results from the smoothie and better health balance from eating whole foods. This will better prepare your body an all-liquid diet.

What you can do to start is to consume two smoothies a day, but round out your diet with a whole foods snack or a whole foods dinner. Just remember that a smoothie is not a dessert. It is and should be a meal replacement.

What to Eat:

- **Beans** – Black beans are recommended, but any bean would do. Make a simple black bean chili or soup in a large quantity so you can eat it for days. They are healthy and easy to eat.

- **Steamed Veggies** – You already know it. These are a must for any health dish. Just add a pinch of salt and/or pepper and you're good.

- **Quinoa** – A perfect protein source, just a cup and a half of this grain cooked provides 12.2 grams of protein. It's easy to prepare and can be flavored. many way. Just use your imagination.

What to Avoid:

- **Frozen Food** – A lot of these are high in sodium, and freezing make them definitely less nutritious.

- **Canned Goods** – Also high in sodium, they also contain other chemicals such as preservatives, which are unhealthy and can be dangerous to your health.

Fat Burning Smoothie Recipes

Now, we've come to the most exciting part of our little journey – smoothie making time! Because I am extremely proud of you for choosing the healthy way to lose weight, I will share with you my all-time favorite fat-burning smoothie recipes.

I lost extra pounds while remaining healthy because of these mouth-watering concoctions, that's why they remain close to my heart. Some of these recipes I got from both my health-conscious mother and grandmother, some I concocted on my own throughout years of blending and juicing.

From many years ago to this day, my family, my friends, friends of friends and even their families have commended me for my delicious fat-burning smoothie recipes, which have helped them all in their weight-loss journeys.

I am happy to share them with you as well, and I hope they'll be of great help to you on your weight loss journey, too.

Vegetable Smoothies

Vegetables, especially leafy greens, are versatile, highly nutritious and are effective weight-loss aids. They contain very few calories and carbohydrates, yet they provide countless much-needed vitamins and minerals.

Veggies also provide the body with sufficient amounts of Vitamins B, C, K, folic acid and other important vitamins. Vitamin deficiency leads to an increased appetite so vegetable smoothies are your friend when you want to lose those extra pounds.

Aside from green leafy veggies, here are some of the most commonly used vegetables used in smoothies and their value in calories *per piece*:

- Carrot: 30 calories
- Pumpkin (1 cup, mashed): 49 calories
- Cucumber: 45 calories
- Tomato (technically a fruit): 33 calories
- Broccoli (1 cup, chopped): 31 calories
- Eggplant: 132 calories
- Beetroot: 35 calories
- Onion: 46 calories
- Garlic (1 clove): 4 calories

- Bell Pepper (technically a fruit): 31 calories

- Fennel (bulb): 14 calories

Below I provide some of my favorite vegetable smoothie recipes, meaning the ingredients are mostly vegetables. Have fun!

Green Smoothie for the Newbie

This recipe is one of the first smoothies I ever consumed back when I started my first ever smoothie diet. Though I was fond of eating veggies, I know not all of you are. This is a good start if you want a good 'ol vegetable smoothie.

Spinach is always a good place to start with a vegetable smoothie. Apart from its soft texture and mild flavor, it is considered to be one of the most nutritious foods in the world. Packed full of iron, calcium, fiber, and plenty of vitamins and minerals, a spinach-based smoothie will do nothing but good for both your health and your weight.

Ingredients:

1 cup baby spinach leaves (7 calories)

1 cup swiss chard (7 calories)

1/4 cup kale (8.25 calories)

1 small banana, frozen (72 calories)

1 tsp. ground flaxseeds (13 calories)

A dash of cinnamon

Purified water

4-5 ice cubes

Total Calories: 107.25

Seargent Pepper

Adding bell peppers to your green smoothies is a great way to add flavor. Red, green and orange bell peppers are good weight loss aids on top of being very nutritious.

A medium-sized red bell pepper provides you with nearly twice the RDA for Vitamin C. These flavorful fruits are also rich in B vitamins, niacin, thiamine, riboflavin, manganese, protein, fiber and antioxidants.

I usually drink this delicious green smoothie during lunch. The Vitamin C from the bell peppers gives me energy for the rest of the day!

Ingredients:

1 red bell pepper, seeded (31 calories)

1/2 green bell pepper, seeded (15.5 calories)

1 cup spinach (7 calories)

1/2 cup avocado slices (117 calories)

1 tomato (33 calories)

1 clove garlic (4 calories)

Purified water

5-6 ice cubes

Total Calories: 207.5

El Zucchini

Zucchini is one of the most refreshing vegetables. That's why it's popular during the summer even though it's available for most of the year.

One thing I like about this veggie is how easily you can prepare it. Plus, it's a great diet food! It's very low in calories, so even if you consume a sizeable portion, you don't take in too many calories.

Enjoy this mouth-watering veggie smoothie!

Ingredients:

1/2 medium zucchini, grated (15.5 calories)

2 cups spinach (14 calories)

1/2 cup mango slices (49.5 calories)

1 cup unsweetened soy milk (90 calories)

1 tsp, agave nectar (21 calories)

5 raw pistachio kernels (20 calories)

5-6 icc cubes

Total Calories: 210

Morning Tropical Smoothie

Like I mentioned above, leafy greens are not only good for your health, but they're good for maintaining a healthy weight as well.

Kale is an excellent source of plant-based calcium while Celery has anti-inflammatory properties and is known to be an effective cholesterol buster. Now, for a sweet and tangy twist, add some pineapple. Pineapples are one of the sweetest fruits out there, but contain many fewer calories than your usual sugary desserts.

Drink this delicious vegetable smoothie on a hot afternoon and you'll certainly feel refreshed.

Ingredients:

1/2 cup kale (16.5 calories)

1 medium stalk celery (6 calories)

1/2 cup fresh or frozen pineapple (45 calories)

1/2 tsp. bee pollen (8.5 calories)

1 dash turmeric (1 calorie)

3 dashes ginger powder (1 calorie)

Purified water

5-6 ice cubes

Total Calories: 78

Fresher than Fresh Smoothie

Did some light exercises to help get rid of those extra pounds? I know you must be thirsty and I've got just the right vegetable smoothie for you to drink.

This recipe makes use of swiss chard, another nutrient-packed leafy green. It contains high amounts of Vitamins A, C and K as well as iron, magnesium, manganese and potassium. It is mildly salty in flavor, which will help cut the sweetness of fruit ingredients.

Cucumber is another important ingredient in this recipe. It is made up of 95 percent water, which will help hydrate your body after completing an exercise routine. This weight-loss vegetable recipe is fresher than fresh!

Ingredients:

1 cup swiss chard (7 calories)

1 medium cucumber (25 calories)

2 medium celery stalks (12 calories)

8 pcs. green grapes (16 calories)

2 mint leaves

Purified water

4-5 ice cubes

Total calories: 60

Smoothie Zing

If you want to take a break from leafy greens, this is what I recommend. Believe it or not, when I'm on an all-smoothie diet and there's a party at home, this is what I drink while everyone else sips cocktails. I especially love its spicy twist! While I get to enjoy this delicious smoothie, I also get to watch my health and my weight.

The recipe is comprised of different colors of vegetables, which experts recommend so that you get maximum nutrients.

Ingredients:

1 zucchini (31 calories)

6 cherry tomatoes (18 calories)

1 large red bell pepper (30 calories)

2 white onion slices (12 calories)

4 medium celery stalks (24 calories)

1 tsp. chili powder (8 calories)

1 tsp. ground flaxseeds (13 calories)

Purified water

Total Calories: 136

Sweet Pumpkin Smoothie

Personally, I am a big fan of pumpkin – I love its taste, texture, and all the benefits I get from eating it. Pumpkins contain Vitamins A, B-6, C and E as well as iron, magnesium and phosphorus. They're also ideal for weight loss because they are low in calories, rich in dietary fiber and contain no fat or cholesterol.

Combine with some veggies like carrots and spinach and you'll have a glassful of thick, creamy goodness.

Ingredients:

1 cup pumpkin, freshly-cooked and cooled, mashed (49 calories)

1/2 cup carrots, chopped (26.5 calories)

2 cups baby spinach (14 calories)

1/4 tsp. nutmeg (3 calories)

1 tsp. ground cinnamon (6 calories)

1 cup unsweetened almond milk (40 calories)

Total Calories: 138.5

Veggie Salad in a Glass

Even though you can eat fresh salad while on a smoothie diet, why not try something new and drink your salad instead? Imagine all those leafy greens, tomatoes and herbs in one glass of nutritious goodness.

I drink this delicious vegetable smoothie as a meal replacement, usually for lunch. The Vitamin C from tomatoes boosts my energy and recharges me for the rest of the day!

Ingredients:

2 large red or yellow tomatoes (64 calories)

1 large carrot (30 calories)

1/2 cup kale (16.5 calories)

1/2 cup parsley (11 calories)

1/2 cup basil (12 calories)

Purified water

4-5 ice cubes

Total Calories: 133.5

Veggie Yummy!

Who doesn't love tomatoes? They're rich in calcium, iron, copper, fluoride, sodium, magnesium, phosphorus, potassium and zinc (whew!). Though actually a fruit, tomatoes are more widely used as a vegetable.

According to the USDA's Nutrient Base, tomatoes contain both mono- and polyunsaturated fats which help control cholesterol levels, support weight loss and are good for the heart.

Add some leafy greens, carrots and spices and you're sure to love this vegetable smoothie as much as I do,

Ingredients:

6 cherry tomatoes (18 calories)

3 small carrots (63 calories)

1 cup baby spinach (7 calories)

1 clove garlic (4 calories)

1 tsp. dill (6 calories)

2 tbsp. balsamic vinegar (28 calories)

A dash of salt

Purified water

Total Calories: 126

Hot and Spicy Smoothie

Contrary to popular belief, not all smoothies are sweet and milkshake-like. If you're creative and adventurous, you'll never run out of ingredients for veggie smoothies.

I got this recipe from my grandmother. I was hesitant to try it but once I did, I couldn't get enough of its spicy goodness! It's a perfect choice to take a break from sweet and fruity smoothies.

Believe it or not, chili peppers can be a great addition to weight loss smoothies. Studies at Laval University in Canada show capsaicin the chemical that gives chili its pungency, helps curb appetite and increases the body's ability to burn fat.

Heat up a cold night with this unique vegetable smoothie!

Ingredients:

1 hot chili pepper (18 calories)

1 large red tomato (32 calories)

1 large carrot (30 calories)

1 cup kale (33 calories)

1 lemon, peeled (17 calories)

Purified water

Total Calories: 130

Broccoli Surprise

Unlike me, many people don't like broccoli very much. You should know that broccoli is another superfood packed with vital nutrients – Vitamins A, B vitamins and C, folate, calcium, iron, fiber, protein and antioxidants.

Using broccoli in a smoothie is a little tricky because of its somewhat bitter taste, so what I do is freeze it first to lessen the bitterness and make it easier to work with.

Besides, when it comes to smoothies, bitterness is easy to mask. In this recipe, I use honey and banana.

Ingredients:

2 cups broccoli, frozen and chopped (62 calories)

1 medium banana (105 calories)

1 tsp. honey (22 calories)

Purified water

4-5 ice cubes

Total Calories: 189

Sweetest Potato Smoothie

Sweet potato is used in a lot of delicious dishes, but is rarely used as an ingredient in vegetable smoothies (yes, it is a vegetable). Because of its low calorie, high fiber and high water content, it is definitely a must for your weight loss smoothies.

To make a creamier consistency for your drink, cook and mash the sweet potato before blending. Enjoy this unique vegetable smoothie to pave your way to a healthier, slimmer body.

Ingredients:

1 cup freshly-cooked and cooled, cubed sweet potato (114 calories)

2 cups lettuce (10 calories)

1/2 tbsp. pecans, chopped (25 calories)

1 cup unsweetened almond milk (40 calories)

1/2 tsp. ground cinnamon (3 calories)

Purified water

5-6 ice cubes

Total Calories: 192

Fruit Smoothies

Fruit smoothies are probably one of the reasons why you decided to go an a smoothie diet for weight loss. They are incredibly delicious and equally healthy. It's like you're not on a diet at all!

Apart from the spectrum of vitamins, minerals and other important nutrients that fruits contain, they are also rich in healthy sugars, healthy carbohydrates, water and dietary fiber – all of which play an important role in any weight loss regime.

According to Mayo Clinic, fruits are low-energy-density food, meaning they provide more volume but less calories. As a result, you will feel full longer, aiding you in your goal to lose weight.

While your body needs calories to function, you have to be extra mindful of what you put in your smoothies if you want to lose those extra pounds. Fruits pack in more calories than vegetables do, so go for fruits that are less calorie dense.

Here is a short list of raw fruits commonly used in smoothies and their value in calories *per piece:*

- Apple:78 calories
- Lemon: 17 calories
- Orange:62 calories
- Banana: 90 calories
- Pear: 51 calories
- Avocado: 322 calories
- Strawberry (1 cup, whole): 47 calories
- Blueberry (1 cup): 85 calories
- Mango: (1 cup) 99 calories
- Pineapple: (1 cup): 82 calories
- Watermelon (1 cup, chopped): 46 calories

Now I will share with you some of my favorite fruit smoothie recipes for weight loss. I hope you enjoy them!

Classic Strawberry

While I do encourage you to be creative with your weight-loss smoothies, it's good to start with the simplest recipes. Besides, nothing beats the classics.

Strawberries are loaded with Vitamin C, calcium, potassium, magnesium and fiber. They have powerful antioxidant and anti-inflammatory properties. But most of all, they are an effective weight loss aid as they help curb appetite and slow down the digestion of starchy foods.

Drink this mouth-watering smoothie for breakfast and you'll feel full until lunch!

Ingredients:

1 cup strawberries (47 calories)

1 cup watermelon, chopped and seeded (46 calories)

1/2 cup plain, low-fat yogurt (77 calories)

4-5 ice cubes

Total Calories: 170

Creamy Guava Smoothie

A guava is yet another refreshing fruit to add to your fruit smoothies. It is rich in Vitamins A, B and C, calcium, iron, potassium, folic acid, nicotinic acid and fiber. Aside from being nutritionally-rich, guavas also aid in weight loss.

Because it is packed full of fiber, guava is a natural laxative, helping you flush out toxins and other impurities from the body, including fat. It also promotes healthy digestion.

So if you're in the mood for something light and creamy, this delectable smoothie is the one to concoct!

Ingredients:

1/2 cup guava nectar (77.5 calories)

1 cup strawberries (47 calories)

1/2 banana, frozen (45 calories)

1/2 cup plain, non-fat yogurt (38.5 calories)

5-6 ice cubes

Total Calories: 208

Vanilla Citrus Delight

Add vanilla extract to any dessert recipe and it will instantly turn delightful. Dieters like me love it because of its low-calorie flavoring and of course, its sweet, delicious taste.

According to the *Reader's Digest* and UK's *The Daily Mail*, the scent of vanilla can help you lose weight by reducing your cravings for sweets. While vanilla is often found in fattening foods such as cake and ice cream, mix it with the right ingredients (like fresh fruits) to help you trim those extra pounds.

Ingredients:

1 cup strawberries (47 calories)

1/2 cup fresh orange juice (55.5 calories)

1/4 cup soft tofu (38 calories)

1 tbsp. raw honey (64 calories)

1/2 tsp. pure vanilla extract (6 calories)

5-6 ice cubes

Total Calories: 210.5

Berry Nutty Peach

Blackberries give a sweet, mild flavor plus they add an interesting crunch because of their tiny seeds. But apart from this, they are very effective weight loss aids.

Blackberries are about 80 percent water, so when you eat them as a snack, you'll feel full longer. These tiny wonder fruits are also very nutritious – they provide 28 percent of the RDA of fiber, 4 percent of calcium, 4 percent of iron and half of the RDA of Vitamin C per cup.

Mix blackberries with other slimming foods like fruits and nuts and you'll instantly have a delicious weight-loss fruit smoothie.

Ingredients:

1 cup blackberries, frozen (62 calories)

1 cup peach slices, frozen (61 calories)

1 tbsp. walnuts (48 calories)

1/4 cup soft tofu (38 calories)

2 tbsp. fresh lemon juice (6 calories)

5-6 ice cubes

Total Calories: 215

Good Morning Sunshine!

This is probably one of my favorite morning smoothies because my husband made me this as a breakfast in bed on my birthday many years ago. Kidding aside, I really love this recipe because kiwi fruit is so refreshing!

It is rich in Vitamin C and fiber while low in calories. According to a clinical nutrition specialist, Dr. Johnny Bowden, kiwi fruit can contribute to weight loss because of their amount of fiber.

Kiwis are also low-glycemic fruit, so they help control your blood sugar levels and maintain them throughout the day. A rise in blood sugar triggers the release of insulin, which could lead to fat storage instead of far burning

Ingredients:

1 ripe kiwi, peeled and quartered (46 calories)

1 cup mango, frozen (99 calories)

1/2 cup organic green tea (0 calories)

1/2 cup low-fat vanilla yogurt (38.5 calories)

1 tsp. raw honey (22 calories)

4-5 ice cubes

Total Calories: 205.5

Dieter's Passion

This yummy egg-shaped tropical fruit is another ingredient you can add to your weight loss smoothies. Also known as purple granadillas, passion fruit is packed with Vitamins A and C, calcium, copper, iron, magnesium, potassium, phosphorus, fiber and protein.

It is known to stimulate digestion, aid gastric ailments, cleanse the colon and contribute to weight loss. Its anti-inflammatory properties will also help you maintain health while shedding those extra pounds.

Ingredients:

1 passion fruit (17 calories)

1/2 banana, frozen (45 calories)

1/2 cup fresh orange juice (55.5 calories)

2 tbsp. non-fat Greek yogurt (16 calories)

1 tbsp. wheat germ (25 calories)

4-5 ice cubes

Total Calories: 158.5

The Sugar Plum Fairy

You probably know the sweet and magical character of the Sugar Plum Fairy, whom everyone adores. When it comes to smoothies, this recipe is her counterpart because well, it is sweet, magical and you'll definitely adore it!

Plums are extremely nutritious – they are rich in Vitamin A, iron, potassium and dietary fiber. They are good for the heart and circulatory system, as well as the digestive system.

These fruits of purple goodness not only contributes to fat burning, but will also help keep you energized throughout the day!

Ingredients:

2 plums, pitted, quartered (60 calories)

1 vanilla bean, seeded (0 calories)

1/2 cup low-fat buttermilk (49.5 calories)

1 tbsp. raw honey (64 calories)

6-7 ice cubes

Total Calories: 173.5 calories

The Miracle Fruit Smoothie

This miracle fruit I'm referring to is soursop, a native of South America, parts of Asia, Africa and the Caribbean. It is called many different names such as guyabano and custard apple.

I immediately fell in love with soursop the first time I tasted it. I call it the 'miracle fruit' because it is best known for its anti-cancer benefits. Soursop is loaded with B vitamins, Vitamin C, folate, calcium, iron, potassium and dietary fiber. Because it helps control blood sugar and contains a good amount of fiber, soursop also helps burn fat.

Enjoy this unique fruit smoothie as well as the health and weight loss benefits it provides.

Ingredients:

1/2 cup soursop chunks (74 calories)

1/4 cup pineapple chunks (20.5 calories)

1 cup unsweetened almond milk (40 calories)

1 tbsp. raw honey (64 calories)

A dash of nutmeg

5-6 ice cubes

Total Calories: 198.5

Blue Banana Smoothie

Bananas are popular ingredients in a fruit smoothie because they give the mixture a creamy texture. Not only that, but this yummy fruit is also a fat-free way to get vitamins such as Vitamin B-6 and C, and minerals like potassium and magnesium, as well as dietary fiber.

Blueberries are also very powerful antioxidants. Just a single serving of this small but wonderful fruit will fill your stomach longer with its fiber content. Another great thing about blueberries is that they are also known to have anti-aging effects!

Ingredients:

1/2 cup blueberries, frozen (42.5 calories)

1 banana, frozen (90 calories)

1/2 cup baby spinach (3.5 calories)

1 tbsp. raw cacao powder (10 calories)

A dash of cayenne pepper

Purified water

4-5 ice cubes

Total Calories: 146

The Great White Smoothie

Power up your morning with this delcious smoothie combining pears, bananas and skim milk. Pears are one of the most versatile fruits there is, plus other fruits pale in comparison to it when it comes down to fiber content.

I really like this smoothie beacuse I'm used to having a glass of low-fat milk in the morning when I'm not on a smoothie diet. The best part of all, one glass of the Great White smoothie provide your body with 28% of fiber's daily value.

Ingredients:

2 pears (102 calories)

1/2 banana (45 calories)

1 tsp. raw ginger root, peeled and coarsely chopped (2 calories)

1 cup skim milk (86calories)

5-6 ice cubes

Optional: A dash of cinnamon

Total Calories: 235

Fruitea Smoothie

Green tea is known for the many health benefits it provides the body. But not many people know of its fat-burning properties.

Green tea helps speed up metabolism and helps rid the body of impurities. It also contains an antioxidant called catechin which stimulates the nervous system and promotes weight-loss.

Drink this refreshing flavor of fruity goodness plus the many benefits of green tea, all in one glass!

Ingredients:

1 cup organic green tea (0 calories)

1 pear (51 calories)

3 tbsp. fresh lemon juice (9 calories)

2 tsp. agave nectar (42 calories)

2 tbsp. plain, fat-free Greek yogurt (35 calories)

5-6 ice cubes

Total Calories: 137

Soy and Berry Smoothie

I like to give my smoothies variety, so sometimes instead of plain milk, I use unsweetened soy milk. Compared to regular milk, soy milk has reduced calorie and sugar content. It is also packed with good amounts of vitamins, minerals, essential fatty acids and proteins.

Soy milk has monosaturated fat, which inhibits intestinal fat, helps prevent cholesterol absorption and decrease blood fat.

Use this as a base for berries and you're sure to ask for more!

Ingredients:

1 cup blueberries, frozen (85 calories)

1 cup plain, unsweetened soy milk (90 calories)

1 tbsp. raw honey (64 calories)

A dash of nutmeg

5-6 ice cubes

Total Calories: 239

Coco Mango Smoothie

Did you know just one mango can provide an entire day's worth of Vitamin C? Apart from their lovely taste, mangoes are loaded with antioxidant beta carotene and carotenoid lycopene, as well as calcium and magnesium.

A recent Australian shows certain phytochemicals found in mangoes help prevent the growth of human fat cells. Professor Mike Gidley of the University of Queensland, says more work must be done to understand the complex compounds found in mangoes. It was recently discovered that eating the skin of a ripe mango can help burn fat.

Adding pure coconut water will contribute to your weight loss because it's known to increase metabolic rate. It also contains natural vitamins, minerals, salts and sugars.

Something I would recommend if you need an energy booster for a busy day!

Ingredients:

1 cup mango, sliced (99 calories)

1 kiwi (42 calories)

1 cup lettuce, shredded (5 calories)

1 cup pure coconut water (46 calories)

4-5 ice cubes

Total Calories: 192

Nutty Raspberry

Who doesn't love raspberries? These sweet little fruits are low in fat and calories but high in insoluble fiber. They are rich in B vitamins, Vitamin C, copper, iron, folic acid, magnesium and manganese.

Just 1 cup of fresh red raspberries provides you with 50 percent of the RDA for Vitamin C, 60 percent for manganese and 33 percent for fiber.

Raspberries are also among the lowest on the glycemic index. According to Dr. Mabel Blades, low-glycemic foods help control blood sugar levels in the body, making weight loss and weight loss management easier.

Ingredients:

1 cup raspberries, frozen (65 calories)

1/2 banana, frozen (45 calories)

5 pcs. almonds (35 calories)

1 cup unsweetened almond milk (40 calories)

5-6 ice cubes

Total Calories: 185

Note: Fresh berries can be used, if available. If using frozen banana, I recommend you slice it first, so you don't break your blender.

Apple Cucumber Twist

This weight loss fruit smoothie is one of my favorite coolers. I usually drink this on a hot sunny day or after I work out. It's both light and refreshing!

Apples satisfy hunger and help keep you feeling full for just a few calories. Pectin, a soluble fiber found in apples, helps boost digestion and also aids in weight loss. Apart from being very versatile fruits, apples also contain powerful antioxidants.

Cucumbers are good for rehydration. They are also natural diuretics which provide cleansing and weight loss benefits. The Vitamins A, C and E found in cucumbers help rid the body of fat cells and toxins.

Ingredients:

1 apple (78 calories)

1 small cucumber, peeled (20 calories)

1 tbsp. ginger, minced (19 calories)

3 tbsp. fresh lime juice (12 calories)

1 tsp. honey (22 calories)

Purified water

4-5 ice cubes

Total Calories: 151

Cherry Oatmeal Delight

Cherries are best known to everyone as an ice cream topper, but once in a while I like to use them as an ingredient in my fruit smoothies.

According to Consumer Reports, the anthocyanins that cherries contain help lower cholesterol and blood pressure. They are also powerful antioxidants and contain a lot of fiber that contributes to weight loss.

Oatmeal, one of the richest sources of soluble fiber, which you know by now is an important nutrient for losing weight.

Enjoy this mouth-watering, thick creamy goodness of nutrition!

Ingredients:

1 cup cherries, fresh or frozen, without pits (77 calories)

4 tbsp. oats, uncooked, preferably rolled oats (40 calories)

1/2 cup plain, low-fat yogurt (38.5 calories)

1/2 tbsp. chia seeds (30 calories)

1/2 cup skim milk (43 calories)

5-6 ice cubes

Total Calories: 228.5

Minty Papaya Smoothie

Feeling bloated, tired or sluggish? This fruity goodness of a smoothie is just what you need! The ingredients will boost your energy and relieve that bloated feeling.

Papaya is rich in Vitamins A and C as well as folate and potassium. It also contains papain, a unique natural enzyme which speeds up the movement of food through the gut, making the fruit an effective weight loss aid.

Mint is known to relieve upset stomachs, making the combination of these two ingredients a good refresher when you're tired or when you've overindulged.

Ingredients:

1 small papaya, solo or Mexican (67 calories)

1/2 cup plain, low-fat yogurt (38.5 calories)

1/2 tbsp. ginger, finely chopped (9.5 calories)

1/2 tbsp. raw honey (32 calories)

2 tbsp. fresh lemon juice (6 calories)

4 fresh mint leaves

Purified water

4-5 ice cubes

Total Calories: 153

Green Smoothies

The basic definition of green smoothies are leafy greens combined with fruits to make a glassful of nutritious beverage. Ideally, green smoothies are 60% fruit and 40% vegetables.

I know I listed several vegetable smoothies above, but this time, instead of any vegetable, we will combine fruits with leafy greens exclusively.

Leafy greens are rich in fiber which makes them slower to digest, which in turn will help you feel full longer, helping you eat less. They are almost carb-free and have very little impact on blood sugar.

Dark leafy greens are packed full of calcium and iron, which dieters need in order to perform exercises to increase the benefit of their weight-loss regimens.

Here is a short list of raw leafy greens commonly used in smoothies and their value in calories *per cup*:

- Spinach: 7 calories
- Cabbage: 25 calories
- Kale: 33 calories
- Lettuce (shredded): 5 calories
- Swiss chard: 7 calories
- Collard Greens: 11 calories
- Parsley: 22 calories
- Dandelion Greens: 25 calories
- Beet Greens: 8 calories
- Watercress: 4 calories

Enjoy concocting these healthy and heavenly recipes!

Greens N Grapes

Grapes make both delicious snacks and wines. They are nutrition powerhouses, containing vitamins, minerals and many important nutrients, one of which is the antioxidant resveratrol, which has anti-inflammatory properties.

According to a recent study done by the University of Texas Health Science Center and published in the Journal of Biological Chemistry, resveratrol can help manage weight. The antioxidant helps stimulate a hormone called adiponectin, which fights insulin resistance. As a result, it helps us avoid gaining pounds.

Ingredients:

1/2 cup kale (16.5 calories)

1 cup lettuce (5 calories)

1 cup grapes (62 calories)

1 pear (51 calories)

1/2 cup pumpkin, mashed (57.5 calories)

1/2 cup pure coconut water (23 calories)

4-5 ice cubes

Total Calories: 215

Cilantropical!

Cilantro, also known as coriander or chinese parsley, is yet another nutrition powerhouse. It is packed with Vitamins A, B-6, C, E and K as well as the minerals calcium, iron, folate, magnesium, phosphorus, niacin, riboflavin and zinc.

According to Rudolph Ballentine, author of *Diet and Nutrition*, the key to weight loss is to consume foods that are naturally high in vitamins and minerals but relatively low in calories. Cilantro is just the right fit. This wonder herb is also known to encourage proper digestion and movement of the bowel.

This delicious green smoothie recipe also makes use of pineapples. Pineapple is a great alternative to sweet snacks plus it is loaded with Vitamin C!

Ingredients:

1 cup cilantro leaves (4 calories)

1 cup baby spinach (7 calories)

1 cup pineapple chunks, frozen (86 calories)

1/2 banana, frozen (45 calories)

1 tsp. psyllium husk (15 calories)

1 tbsp. chia seeds (60 calories)

A dash of cinnamon

Purified water

5-6 ice cubes

Total Calories: 217

Bok Choy Joy

If you want an exotic addition to your green smoothie, bok choy is definitely a must-try. Bok choy, also referred to as chinese white cabbage, provides a delicious, mild flavor to any dish.

Bok choy is low in calories and carbohydrates but high in essential nutrients. This leafy green is rich in Vitamin C, folic acid, potassium and antioxidants.

So after a moderate workout session, replenish your body with this refreshing green smoothie and you'll finally get to experience bok choy joy!

Ingredients:

1 cup baby bok choy, shredded (11 calories)

2 cups honeydew cubes, frozen (122 calories)

1 tbsp. hemp protein powder (30 calories)

4 mint leaves

Purified water

Total Calories: 163

Rainbow Connection

I always thought of rainbow chard as nature's healthy and colorful surprise. I was a little girl the first time I saw a bunch of it in our kitchen, and I didn't want my mom to cook it because I thought it was pretty!

Sometimes also called 'Bright Lights', rainbow chard is a mix of chard varieties with red, orange, white or yellow stalks. It is highly nutritious, containing good amounts of Vitamins A and C, calcium, iron and dietary fiber.

Maintaining your health is important when you're trying to lose weight. Leafy greens like rainbow chard can help.

Ingredients:

1 cup rainbow chard, shredded (7 calories)

1 cup collard greens (11 calories)

1/2 purple kale (16.5 calories)

1/2 banana, frozen (45 calories)

1/2 cup raspberries, frozen (32.5 calories)

1/2 tsp. ginger (finely chopped)

Purified water

4-5 ice cubes

Total Calories: 112

Fruity VitaWater

Like any other leafy green, watercress doesn't come in last when it comes to nutrition and weight loss benefits. Aside from the wide spectrum of vitamins and minerals that it offers, watercress is known to be the ultimate energy-boosting leafy green.

According to research published in the *British Journal of Nutrition*, watercress has benefits that can supercharge your energy and get you pumped up for your workout.

Concoct this yummy, healthy green smoothie recipe when you have a scheduled workout.

Ingredients:

1 cup watercress (4 calories)

1 cup kale (33 calories)

1 cup mixed berries (60 calories)

1/2 banana (45 calories)

1/2 cup vanilla oat milk (65 calories)

5-5 ice cubes

Total Calories: 207

RED-y for Weight Loss

I know it's quite odd to have an all-reds green smoothie, but did you know that experts call red fruits and vegetables 'the new nutrition powerhouses'?

Many red fruits and veggies contain high amounts of antioxidants like lycopene and anthocyanine as well as a spectrum of vitamins and minerals.

Concoct this delightful red green smoothie and you'll be RED-y to lose those extra pounds!

Ingredients:

1 cup red leaf lettuce, shredded (5 calories)

1/2 beetroot, shredded (17.5 calories)

1 apple (78 calories)

1 /2 cup raspberries, frozen (32.5 calories)

1 cup non-fat greek yogurt (77 calories)

Total Calories: 210

Green Peanut Butter

I never used peanut butter in my smoothies until a few years ago when I read a study from Purdue University (published in the *International Journal of Obesity*) that showed snacking on peanuts as well as peanut butter can help dieters adjust their caloric intake spontaneously.

Peanut butter can help curb hunger effectively, helping you avoid unecessary snacking. Although a little high on calories, peanut butter can provide you with nutrition and weight loss benefits when consumed in moderation.

Besides, it's extremely delicious and hey, you deserve a treat for trying to burn fat the healthy way!

Ingredients:

1 cup kale (33 calories)

1 cup baby spinach (7 calories)

1 cup strawberries (47 calories)

1 tbsp. peanut butter (94 calories)

1 cup unsweetened almond milk (40 calories)

5-6 ice cubes

Total Calories: 221

Tomato and Greens Smoothie

If you want to take a break from sweet smoothies, this is the perfect pick. A combination of leafy greens, a tomato and a cucumber will give you a whole lot of vitamins but a lot less calories – something you want (and need) for shedding those extra pounds.

I like to add some cayenne pepper to this recipe for more depth in taste. Cayenne pepper is best known for helping speed up metabolism. According to the British newspaper *The Sun,* a published study by food scientist Stephen Whiting, shows consuming capsaicin, cayenne's active ingredient, causes an adrenaline rush. This sends a signal to brain to burn fat cells, especially in the stomach area.

Ingredients:

2 cups arugula lettuce (12 calories)

1 cucumber (25 calories)

4 cherry tomatoes (12 calories)

2 tsp. ginger, minced (4 calories)

1 tbsp. cayenne pepper (17 calories)

2 tbsp. fresh lemon juice (6 calories)

Purified water

4-5 ice cubes

Total Calories:76

Raisin' Kale Smoothie

Aside from being heart-friendly, eating raisins can provide more health benefits to the body. According to whfoods.com, these tiny nutrition powerhouses are packed full of antioxidants and promote bone health.

In addition, a recent study done at the University of Connecticut shows that raisins can effectively suppress appetite if eaten as a snack, because they raise leptin levels in the body.

A few raisins combined with leafy greens gives you a smoothie that not only tickles your taste buds, but assists in reaching your weight loss goal as well.

Ingredients:

1 cup kale (33 calories)

1 cup baby spinach (7 calories)

1/4 cup raisins, seedless (108 calories)

1/2 banana (45 calories)

1 tsp. agave nectar (21 calories)

1/2 cup unsweetened almond milk (20 calories)

5-6 ice cubes

Total Calories: 234

Cake Batter Green Smoothie

I call this green smoothie recipe as such because the yummy taste reminds me of cake batter. And who doesn't love cake batter? This weight loss smoothie is one of my favorites and my kids love it, too.

It makes use of figs which may be a calorically-rich fruit, but they are also nutritionally dense. Aside from containing plenty of vitamins, minerals and antioxidants, figs also contain a digestive enzyme called ficin. Ficin promotes healthy digestion and helps move the food you consume through the digestive tract efficiently, which contributes to weight loss.

Ingredients:

2 cups spinach (14 calories)

3 fresh figs, halved (90 calories)

1/2 banana, frozen (45 calories)

1 tsp. honey (22 calories)

1/2 cup vanilla soy milk (45 calories)

4-5 ice cubes

Total Calories: 216

Ooh La Lala!

Here is something to break that monotony and add sometihng new to your smoothie diet.

One way to not feel like you're drinking the same thing voer and over again is to alternate fruit-based with vegetable based smoothies. It's okay to repeat ingredients, but once in a while add in that one ingredient that will your smoothie an extra 'oomph'.

In this case I added jalapeno pepper. Though it may seem unlikely, it actually makes an amazing smoothie when mixed with the right ingredients. According to a 2010 study published in the Nutrition and Metabolism journal, jalapeno peppers contain enzymes called capsinoids that increase calorie burning in the body and promote burning fat to use as fuel.

Ingredients:

1/2 cup collard greens, chopped (5.5 calories)
1 small cucumber, peeled (20 calories)
1/4 avocado (80.5 calories)
1 beetroot (35 calories)
1/2 jalapeno pepper (2 calories)
1 tsp. ginger, finely chopped (2 calories)
2 tbsp. fresh lemon juice (6 calories)
Splash of vanilla extract
5-6 ice cubes

Total Calories: 151

Spinach and Peas Smoothie

I know that by now, you're already used to using spinach and other leafy greens in your weight loss smoothie. But peas are another great green vegetable you can add as an ingredient.

Green peas have a naturally sweet taste which boosts the flavor of your drink. Plus they're loaded with fiber, which researchers have found to help reduce belly fat.

Enjoy this fruitless green smoothie on a busy day or after you workout as it is a natural energy-booster.

Ingredients:

1/4 cup green peas, frozen (29.5 calories)

1 cup spinach (7 calories)

1 cup unsweetened almond milk (40 calories)

2 tsp. ground flaxseeds (26 calories)

1/2 scoop vanilla whey protein powder (60 calories)

4-5 ice cubes

Total Calories: 159.5

The Cool Cactus

If you haven't heard of a nopal or nopales (plural), this is the perfect time for you to include it in your diet. It is basically the pad of the prickly pear cactus and is a common vegetable in Mexico and the southwestern United States.

Nopales contain Vitamins A. B-6 and C as well as minerals calcium, magnesium and sodium. It is low in calories and fat but high in fiber.

I hope you enjoy this refreshingly unique smoothie as much as I did.

Ingredients:

1/2 cup nopal cactus, sliced (7 calories)

1 small cucumber, peeled (20 calories)

1 cup lettuce (5 calories)

1 apple (78 calories)

2 tbsp. fresh lime juice (8 calories)

5-6 ice cubes

Total Calories: 118

Double C Smoothie

I call this green smoothie Double C because it combines the nutritional and weight loss powers of cabbage and cauliflower.

Like any other leafy green, cabbage is naturally high in fiber and low in calories which promotes healthy weight loss. On the other hand, cauliflowers are one of the richest sources of calcium, about 75 percent of the RDA of calcium with every serving. They also contain Vitamin K, fiber, niacin and phosphorus.

Ingredients:

1 cup cabbage, shredded (25 calories)

1/2 cup cauliflower florets (12.5 calories)

1/2 banana (45 calories)

1/2 cup ripe mangoes (49.5 calories)

1 cup plain, unsweetened soy milk (90 calories)

4-5 ice cubes

Total Calories: 222

Lime Pie Smoothie

My family loves lime pies, so I thought of an alternative green smoothie recipe for it. Limes are rich in Vitamin C, which provides the body with plenty of health benefits.

During the first few days of a smoothie fast, some people may experience tiredness or sluggishness because of the change in diet or withdrawal from solid food. That's why a dose of Vitamin C is what you need to boost your energy!

Try this scrumptious smoothie recipe and your family is sure to enjoy it!

Ingredients:

1 cup baby spinach (7 calories)

2 limes (20 calories)

2 tbsp. fresh lime juice (8 calories)

1 banana, frozen (90 calories)

2 pcs. gluten-free graham crackers (60 calories)

1/2 cup unsweetened non-dairy milk (35 calories)

A few drops of vanilla extract

4-5 ice cubes

Total Calories: 220

Mix-Match Smoothie Recipes

These next recipes contain a mix of fruits, vegetables and leafy greens, so I made a special category for them.

They are just as delicious and easy to make as the other ones, and I encourage you to give them all a try.

Berry Eggy Smoothie

Once in a while I mix in an egg or two in my smoothie recipes. Eggs are rich in Vitamins A, B-12, D and E as well as minerals iron, protein and zinc.

In addition, new research shows that eggs promote weight loss. According to a research done at the U.S. Rochester Centre for Obesity, eating eggs for breakfast can help you limit your intake of food by as much as 400 calories throughout the rest of the day.

Ingredients:

1 organic egg (70 calories)

1/2 cup strawberries (23.5 calories)

1/2 cup raspberries (32.5)

1/4 cup coconut meat, shredded (71 calories)

1 cup unsweetened almond milk (40 calories)

4-5 ice cubes

Total Calories: 237

White Bean Smoothie

White beans, sometimes also referred to as white navy beans, are a good thing to add to your weight loss green smoothie. They are very rich sources of fiber, protein and antioxidants.

White beans also rank very low in the glycemic index. They help enzymes from turning simple starches into sugars, which in turn prevents fat storage.

Another awesome thing about using white beans in a smoothie is that you can hardly tell there are beans in your drink, making them a versatile ingredient that you can mix in with other fruits and veggies.

Ingredients:

1/4 cup white beans, canned (77 calories)

1 cup peaches, sliced (61 calories)

1/2 cup rice milk (60 calories)

1/2 tsp. cinnamon (3 calories)

4-5 icc cubes

Total Calories: 201

Cheese and Corn Smoothie

Everybody loves cheesy corn as a side to a meal, but on a smoothie? Yes, I've tried it and it's delicious! Contrary to popular belief, certain kinds of cheese are actually good for weight loss and weight management. Some of the healthiest cheeses that are good for weight loss include low-fat or non-fat varieties of cottage, feta, Parmesan and Swiss cheese.

According to a study done at Australia's Curtin University of Technology, the protein found in cheese is filling and will help you feel less hungry after consumption. In addition, its calcium content boosts metabolism. Always opt for low-fat or low-calorie cheese variety.

On the other hand, corn is naturally high in fiber and is known to curb appetite.

Ingredients:

1/2 cup yellow sweet corn kernels (62.5 calories)

1/2 cup non-fat cottage cheese (52.5 calories)

1/4 avocado (80.5 calories)

1 cup spinach (7 calories)

1 tbsp. fresh lime juice (4 calories)

Purified water

4-5 ice cubes

Total Calories: 206.5

Creamy Pumpkin Cashew

Many dieters avoid eating cashews and other nuts because of their fat content. However, recent research done at the Harvard School of Public Health's Department of Nutrition showed that including nuts into your diet may help with weight control as opposed to contributing to weight gain.

Cashews are one of the healthiest nuts around. They are loaded with zinc, copper, phosphorus, magnesium, and manganese, as well as other important nutrients.

Ingredients:

1 cup pumpkin, freshly-cooked and cooled, mashed (49 calories)

10 pcs. raw cashews (90 calories)

1/2 sliced banana, frozen (45 calories)

1 cup unsweetened almond milk (40 calories)

1/2 tsp. cinnamon (3 calories)

A dash of Celtic sea salt

4-5 ice cubes

Total Calories: 227

The Tropical Tofu

Tofu is a popular food choice for vegetarians and those following a vegetarian diet like it because it's so versatile. According to an interesting study in *Cancer Management and Research* published in 2011, vegetarians generally weigh less (around three to 20 percent less) and have lower risk of obesity compared to those who eat meat.

I figured that tofu would give a thick, creamy texture when mixed in with fruits in smoothies and I was right! And because tofu is naturally loaded with protein, I didn't feel hungry until several hours later after I drank a glass of this refreshing smoothie.

I also used mangoes and pineapple juice for this recipe, which gave me an energy boost because of their Vitamin C content!

Ingredients:

1/2 cup soft tofu (75.5 calories)

1 cup mango, sliced (99 calories)

1/2 cup pineapple chunks (41 calories)

3 tbsp. fresh lime juice (12 calories)

5-6 ice cubes

Total Calories: 227.5

The Quick Refresher

I love refreshing smoothies. We often mistake thirst for hunger, so drinks like this one should be at the top of your list, especially on a warm day.

In this recipe, I used kombucha tea, which is rich in B vitamins and contain minerals such as iron, potassium, phosphorus and chromium. It is also known to help boost energy and speed up metabolism, so all in all it is good for weight loss. Kombucha tea tastes a little bit like apple cider, but it comes in different flavors.

You can find this healthy tea in the refrigerated teas section in local health food stores, well-stocked supermarkets or online.

Ingredients:

1 cup kombucha tea, ginger flavor (30 calories)

1 cucumber, peeled (25 calories)

2 pcs. kiwi, peeled (92 calories)

1/2 cup plain low-fat yogurt (77 calories)

1/4 cup fresh cilantro leaves (1 calorie)

5-6 ice cubes

Total Calories: 225

Prune-Mango Madness

Prunes or dried plums are natural weight loss foods. Although a little heavy on the calorie side, these sweet little nutrition powerhouses are still a friend to dieters.

Full of powerful antioxidants, vitamins and minerals, prunes are also known to be a natural laxative. That's why they are good for digestion and help prevent constipation problems.

The sweetness of prunes can be a great addition to your diet smoothies, so try this recipe and see the results for yourself.

Ingredients:

5 pcs. dried prunes (100 calories)

1/2 cup mango, frozen (49.5 calories)

1 cup spinach (7 calories)

1/2 cup plain low-fat yogurt (77 calories)

5-6 ice cubes

Total Calories: 233.5

It's A Date!

Dates may be high on calories, but they're nutritious and delicious, so I don't have second thoughts about using them as ingredients for my smoothies.

Dates are packed with Vitamins A, B vitamins and C, fiber and protein. Because of their sugar content, dates are also natural energy-boosters.

For this recipe, I used Deglet Noor dates mainly because they have fewer calories and less sugar than the Medjool variety.

So if you're feeling sluggish, boost your energy by drinking this one-of-a-kind smoothie. It's a date!

Ingredients:

1/4 cup Deglet Noor dates, pitted (104 calories)

1/2 cup kale (16.5 calories)

1/2 banana, frozen (45 calories)

1 cup unsweetened almond milk (40 calories)

5-6 ice cubes

Total Calories: 205.5

Spiked Melon Cooler

Melons are juicy fruits that have a naturally sweet taste which makes it easy to combine with different types of produce. This low-calorie, nutritionally-dense fruit is loaded with Vitamins A and C, B vitamins, omega-3s, copper, magnesium, potassium, folate and fiber.

Also, it only takes about 15 to 30 minutes to digest a melon, which makes it good for detox and weight loss.

Ingredients:

1 cup melon cubes (54 calories)

1/2 kiwi, peeled and chopped (23 calories)

1/2 banana, frozen (45 calories)

1 cup watercress (4 calories)

1 tbsp. ginger, minced (19 calories)

Purified water

5-6 ice cubes

Total Calories: 145

Pickled Apple Smoothie

When you go the grocery store, you always see a jar of pickles next to bottles of ketchup and other sauces in the condiments section, and not in the produce or natural foods section.

It is because we have always viewed pickles only as taste enhancers to dishes and not as a meal or a snack by themselves. I love pickles, but some people may not like them. The truth is, they will be of great help when you're on a diet,

Pickes are super low in fat and calories plus pickle juice is rich in electrolytes that help rejuvenate the body. So even if you're not exactly a fan of pickles, give this weight loss smoothie a try and it might change your mind.

Ingredients:

1/2 cup dill pickle slices (9.5 calories)

1 cup apple slices (57 calories)

1 tbsp. fresh lime juice (4 calories)

1 tsp. raw honey (22 calories)

Purified water

4-5 ice cubes

Total Calories: 92.5

Leafy Green Mango Tango

I have shared a lot of sweet smoothie recipes with you, so I thought of adding one that is in the not-too-sweet variety.

This recipe is a simple mix of leafy greens with the sweet and tangy taste of mangoes. I already mentioned the benefits of these ingredients in the recipes above, and I just wanted to share this nutritionally-dense smoothie that is good for any time of the day.

After all, everyone needs a simple, go-to smoothie recipe once in a while.

Ingredients:

1 1/2 cup mangoes, sliced (148.5)

1 cup cilantro leaves (4 calories)

1 cup stinging nettles (37 calories)

1/2 cup dandelion greens (12.5 calories)

3 stalks celery (6 calories)

2 tbsp. fresh lemon juice (6 calories)

Purified water

4-5 ice cubes

Total Calories: 214

Apricot and Spinach Mix

Apricots are rich in both soluble and insoluble fiber. The soluble fiber promotes heart health while the latter promotes weight loss by contributing to a feeling of fullness.

These delicious fruits are also brimming with importants nutrients such as Vitamins A and C, beta-carotene and antioxidants. Combine with spinach (one of the healthiest foods in the world) and you've got yourself a delightful, healthy and slimming green smoothie.

Ingredients:

1 cup apricot halves (75 calories)

2 cups baby spinach (14 calories)

1 cup plain, non-fat yogurt (77 calories)

1 tsp. raw honey (22 calories)

5-6 ice cubes

Total Calories: 188

Final Recommendations

Before I end this book, I'd like to give you some final tips to help you successfully lose weight with a smoothie fast.

Set a goal and stick to it

People go through a smoothie fast for a variety of reasons – to lose weight, to start eating healthy or to generally improve overall health. In your case, you know you are doing this to lose weight.

It's a huge step. So every time you get hungry and feel the need to break your fast, think about your goal and the reward waiting for you at the end of the rainbow.

Start small

It's easy to get excited about a new diet, knowing it could possibly be the answer to your weight loss goals. Because of this, it's also easy to overdo it.

The key here is to start small – slow but sure steps will help you get closer to success.

Even though smoothies are easy to love, it's not exactly easy to all of a sudden give up all the unhealthy solid foods we've grown accustomed to.

Start by drinking one glass of green smoothie a day, supplementing along with healthy solid foods while you slowly remove any unhealthy food that could keep you from reaching your goal.

As your diet becomes healthier, introduce bigger quantities of smoothies until you can drink them as meal replacements.

Start with your favorite fruit and vegetables

Everyone needs time to adjust and familiarize themselves with a new diet.

If you weren't previously a healhy eater, start with fruits and vegetables you do eat once in a while. You know which combinations you like best and can eventually introduce other types of produce you wouldn't normally eat as you become accustomed to the smoothie diet.

Go for variety

I know I've been giving you reminders about this all throughout the book, so I guess you know by now how important variety is to a smoothie diet.

There are literally thousands of weight loss foods out there and each one has different vitamins, minerals and other nutrients to offer. So if you really want to lose weight the healthy way, go for different colors, tastes and textures of produce and other healthy foods to make sure you are maximizing your diet to have a healthier, more fit body.

A smoothie fast is just the beginning

Your journey is just beginning. Think of a smoothie fast as your gateway to a healthier, happier life.

Losing weight is only the first step; everything else comes down to how you're going to maintain the weight you lost.

Create a daily exercise routine that works for you and start eating healthy if you don't want to end up back at square one.

So there you have it! I think you're just about ready to begin.

Remember, nothing and no one can help you with your situation but YOU. You hold the key to your health and happiness, so it's up to you which door you open with it.

In my case, smoothies paved the way to a life that I never thought I could have. I've never been healthier and happier, and I wish that a month or two from now, you will be saying the same thing.

Enjoy the smothie recipes! You can thank me later. Good luck!

About the Author

Donna Hardin is a true believer of the alternative medicine and the wonderful benefits it provides.

She adopted a healthy life style over 10 years ago when she decided to go against the wave and stop eating any processed foods, canned foods or anything containing additives and other harmful chemicals.

She enjoys helping others discover the amazing effects of a healthy diet, whether it is a detox, cleansing, weight loss or any other type of diet.

One of her secrets for a healthy life and a perfect body is fresh juices and smoothies, made out of organic fruits and vegetables. Her favorite quote is "Chew your Drink and Drink your Food".

Check out her other books available on Amazon.com

Other Books by Donna Hardin

1. Juicing Recipes for Weight Loss: Lose Weight, Gain Energy & Improve Health with Delicious Juice Recipes

2. Detox Foods Demystified: The Secrets of the Best Detox Foods & How to Detox Your Body the Right Way

You can connect with Donna on her facebook page:

www.facebook.com/HealthyDietDaily

where she shares daily tips and advice on how to eat healthy on a daily basis.

You can also visit her site:

www.HealthyDietDaily.com

to discover more delicious smoothie and juice recipes, as well as various tips and advice on weight loss diets and how to maintain a healthy lifestyle.

© 2013 by Donna Hardin
All Rights Reserved.

Printed in the United States of America

Made in the USA
Middletown, DE
29 March 2017